2.0

CHILDREN'S ROOM

W9-CTC-270

Awesome Birds
Puffins

Leo Statts

abdopublishing.com

Published by Abdo Zoom, a division of ABDO, P.O. Box 398166, Minneapolis, Minnesota 55439.

Copyright © 2018 by Abdo Consulting Group, Inc. International copyrights reserved in all countries.

No part of this book may be reproduced in any form without written permission from the publisher.

Printed in the United States of America, North Mankato, Minnesota.

092017

012018

THIS BOOK CONTAINS
RECYCLED MATERIALS

Photo Credits: Shutterstock

Production Contributors: Kenny Abdo, Jennie Forsberg, Grace Hansen, John Hansen

Design Contributors: Dorothy Toth, Neil Klinepier

Publisher's Cataloging-in-Publication Data

Names: Statts, Leo, author.

Title: Puffins / by Leo Statts.

Description: Minneapolis, Minnesota: Abdo Zoom, 2018. | Series: Awesome birds |
      Includes online resource and index.

Identifiers: LCCN 2017939232 | ISBN 9781532120619 (lib.bdg.) | ISBN 9781532121739 (ebook) |
      ISBN 9781532122293 (Read-to-Me ebook)

Subjects: LCSH: Puffins--Juvenile literature. | Birds--Juvenile literature.

Classification: DDC 598.33--dc23

LC record available at https://lccn.loc.gov/2017939232

Table of Contents

Puffins 4

Body. 6

Habitat. 12

Food. 16

Life Cycle 18

Quick Stats. 20

Glossary. 22

Online Resources. 23

Index 24

Puffins

There are three types of puffins. They are the Atlantic, horned, and tufted puffins.

A group of puffins is called a colony.

Body

Puffins are covered in feathers. They help them stay warm.

Their feathers are black and white. They change color in the spring.

Puffins have **webbed** feet. Their **beaks** are large and triangle-shaped.

Their beaks are also called bills. Bills are colorful for most of the year.

Habitat

Puffins live on water and land. They can swim, walk, and fly.

In the spring and summer they live on **coasts**. The rest of the time they live at sea.

Food

Puffins are **carnivores**.

Puffins mostly eat small fish. They also eat other types of sea life, like crabs, squids, and urchins.

Life Cycle

Wild puffins can live for more than 20 years.

18

Female puffins lay one egg at a time. They dig a **burrow** near the ocean. Parents feed their **chicks** as they grow.

Average Height

An Atlantic puffin is taller than a basketball.

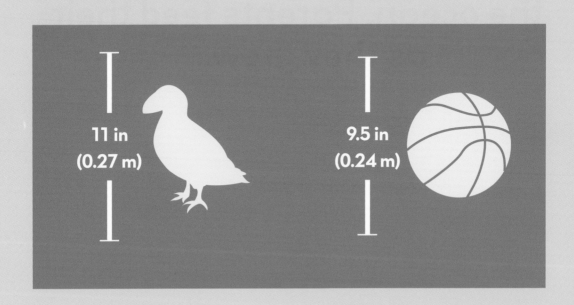

11 in
(0.27 m)

9.5 in
(0.24 m)

Average Weight

A puffin weighs more that four sticks of butter.

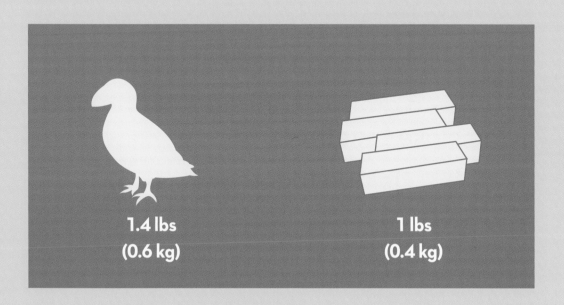

1.4 lbs
(0.6 kg)

1 lbs
(0.4 kg)

Glossary

beak – a hard mouthpart that sticks out.

burrow – an animal's underground home.

carnivore – an animal that eats meat.

chick – a baby bird.

coast – land near a body of water.

colony – a group of animals of one kind living close together.

webbed – joined together by skin.

Online Resources

Booklinks
NONFICTION NETWORK
FREE! ONLINE NONFICTION RESOURCES

For more information on puffins, please visit **abdobooklinks.com**

Abdo Zoom
DATABASES
BEGINNING ONLINE RESEARCH

Learn even more with the Abdo Zoom Animals database. Visit **abdozoom.com** today!

Index

beaks 9, 10

burrow 19

chicks 19

colony 5

color 7, 10

eggs 19

feathers 6, 7

feet 9

food 16, 17, 19

lifespan 18

sea 13, 14, 19